First Christmas

American Sign Language

Eimiko Murlin

A long time ago, there was a girl named Mary

And a **boy** named Joseph.

Mary and Joseph
were going to be
married.

Married
Your dominant hand on top of your
other hand clasping them together

Before the wedding, an angel came to Mary

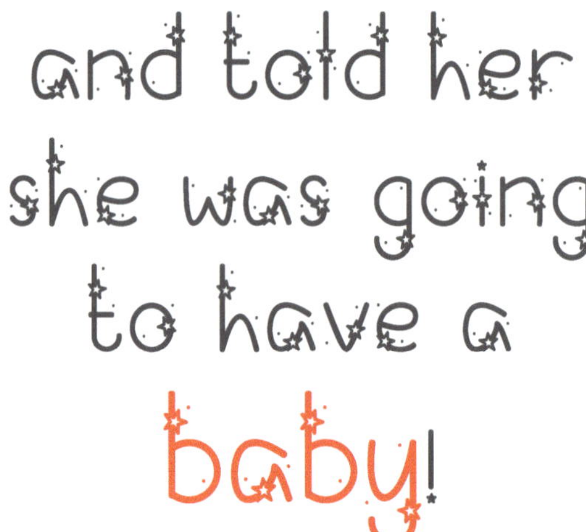

and told her
she was going
to have a
baby!

Baby
Arms on top of each other in
front of you, pretend like your
cradling a baby

The angel said she should name the baby Jesus. The baby would be the Son of God, the Savior.

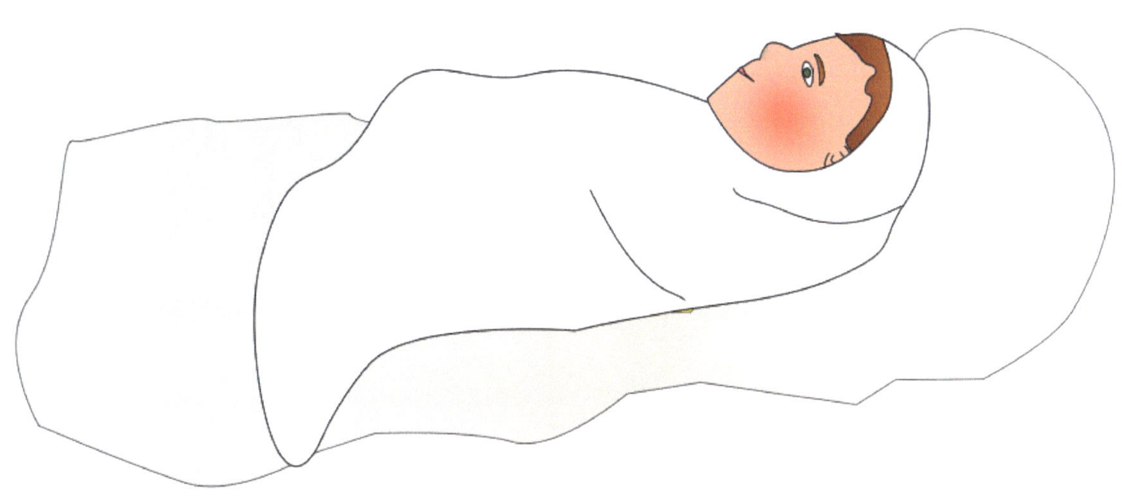

Mary and Joseph had to **go** to a town called Bethlehem.

The town was very crowded. So Mary and Joseph spent the *night* in a barn with the animals.

Night

One hand flat in front of you, the other hand goes over, like the moon going down.

Baby Jesus was born in the barn!
"B" hand shap
Barn
Using "B" hands, show the shape of a barns roof and walls

A new bright star appeared in the sky over the barn.
Star
Both pointer fingers go up and down past each other, like pointing to the stars in the sky

Shepherds were taking care of sheep in nearby fields..

An Angel came and told the shepherds that the Savior had been born

The shepherds went to find and worship the baby Jesus.

Find
Thumb and pointer finger, pointing down left hand while pinching them together. Three fingers are straight out

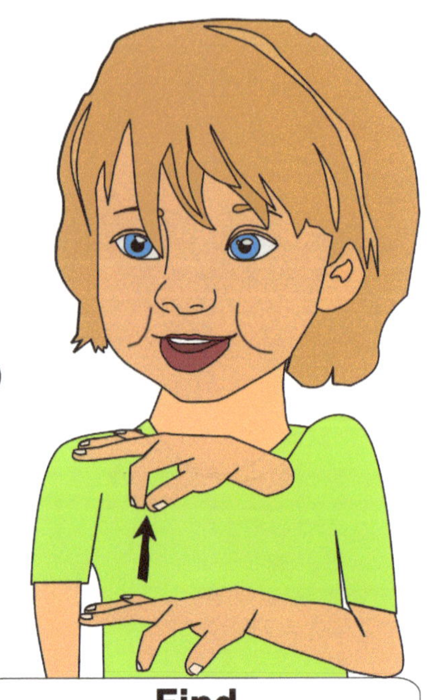

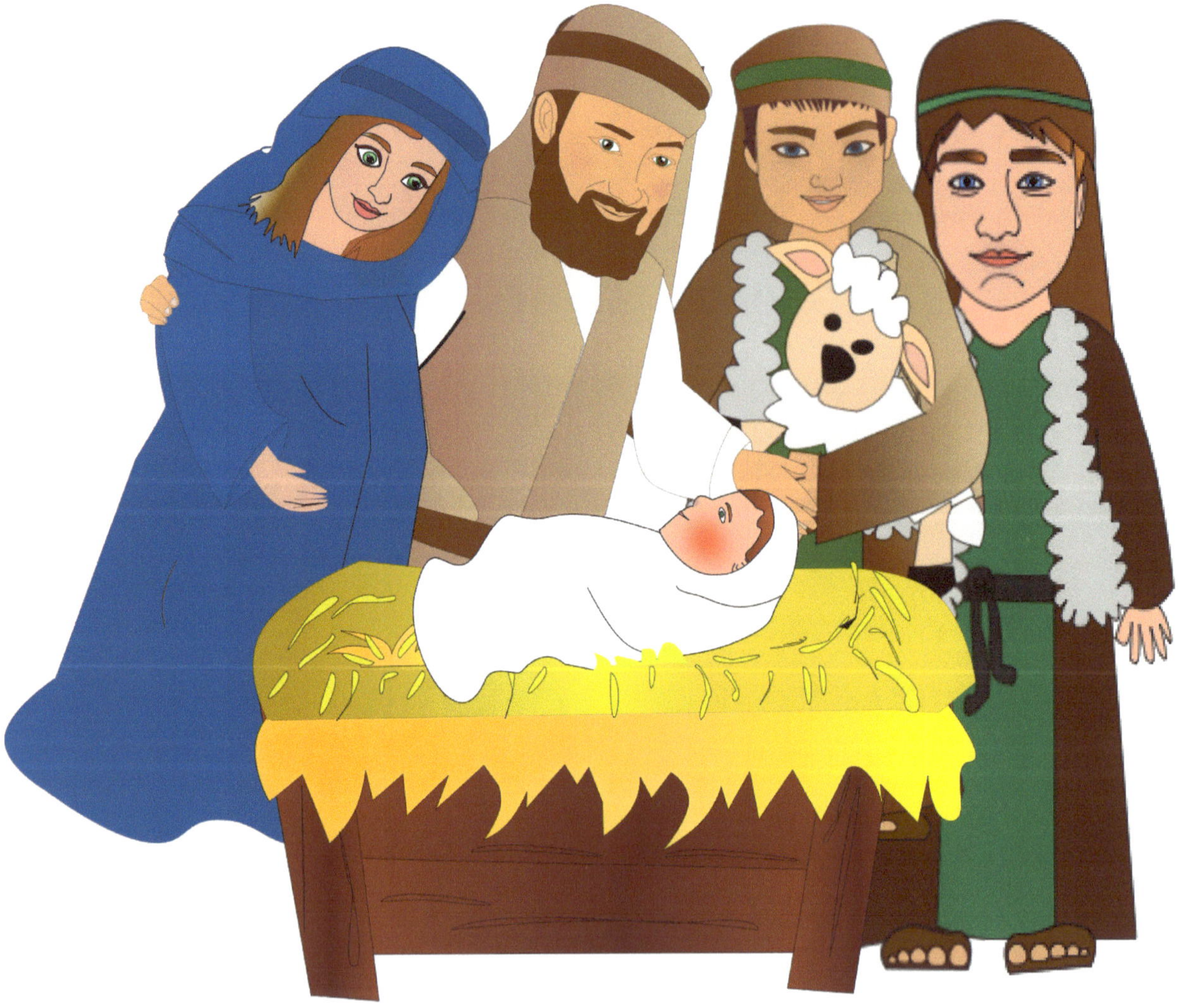

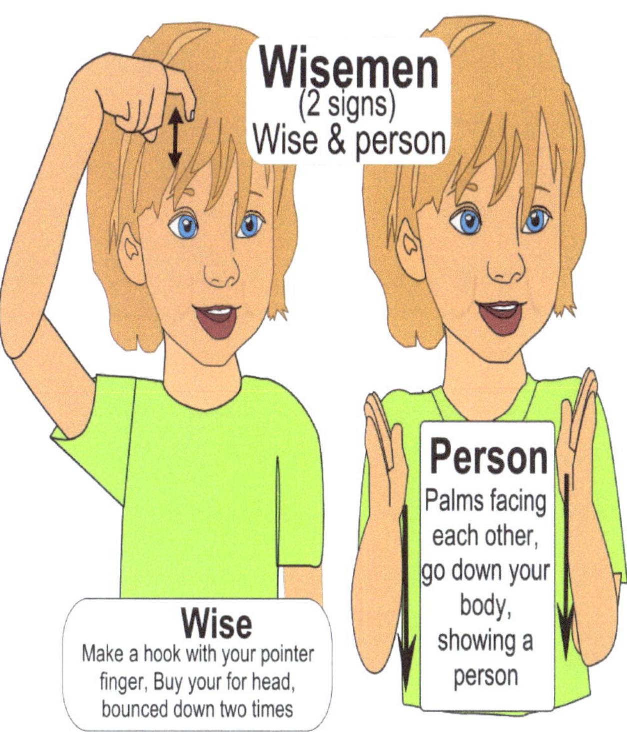

Far away, Wise Men saw the new star. They knew it was a sign that the Savior had been born.

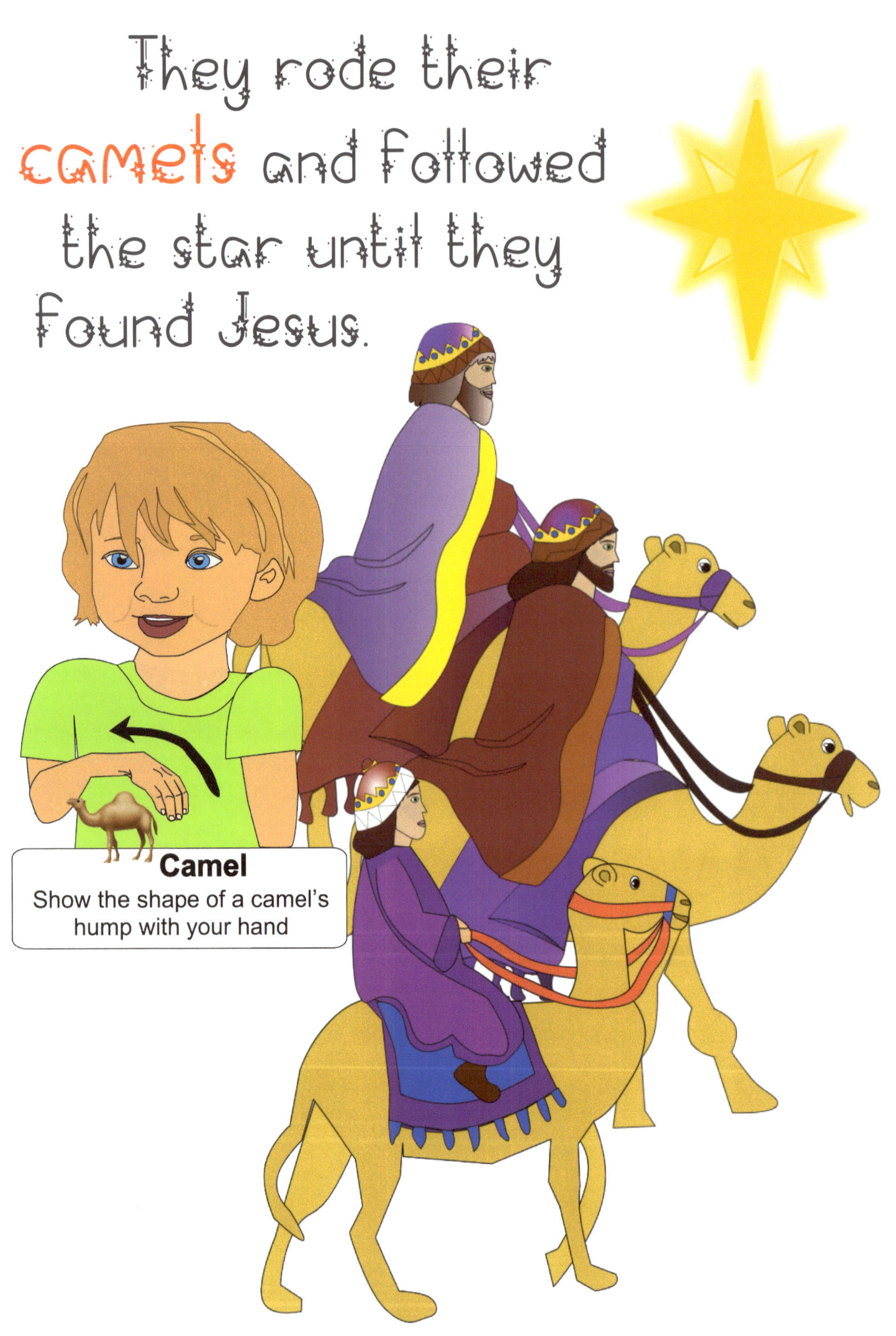

They rode their camels and followed the star until they found Jesus.
Camel
Show the shape of a camel's hump with your hand

They gave Him gifts and worshipped Him.

After the Wise Men said goodbye,

an angel told Joseph a **bad** king wanted to hurt Jesus.

Bad
Make a gross, face touch your lips, your hand down and away, Palm facing down, like putting something bad out of your mouth

The angel said
their Family
should move to
Egypt to be safe.

Family
Both hands touching at the
index fingers and thumbs,
circle the two hands
around, ending with the
pinkie fingers touching

Joseph, Mary, and Jesus lived in Egypt until it was safe to return to Israel. Jesus grew up in a town called Nazareth.

He learned to be helpful, kind, and obedient. He always followed God's plan for Him.

Help
Put your closed-fist on top of your other hands open palm, and move both hands upwards.

At Christmas we celebrate the birth of Jesus.
Point to the pictures of the people. who were part of the story.
~Find Mary and Joseph
We can be like Mary and Joseph by doing what God wants us to do.
~ Find the shepherds
We can be like the shepherds and listen to what God says.
~Find the Wise Men
We can be like the Wise Men by Following Jesus Christ.
~Find the angel
We can be like the angel by telling others the real story of Christmas.
~Find Jesus
And we can be like Jesus by Following His ways!

The

End

Outside set 1

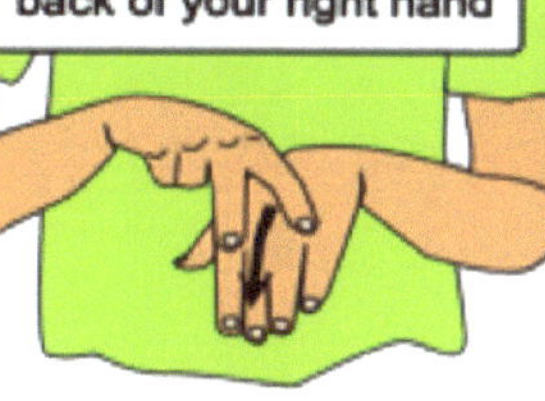

Outside
Open hand at your for head, move hand away & closing your fingers

Slide
Two fingers on your left hand slide down the back of your right hand

Run
Hook your pointer finger around your thumb, move them forward.

Kite
Palm up is the kite, pointer finger is the string.

Walk
Both palms open, facing towards the ground, back-and-forth like walking

Ball
Pretend like you're holding a ball, move your hands together and apart, Showing the shape

Swing
two fingers, on top of right two fingers, move back-and-forth, like swinging

Bike
fists in front, like peddling a bike

ASL Counting 1-20

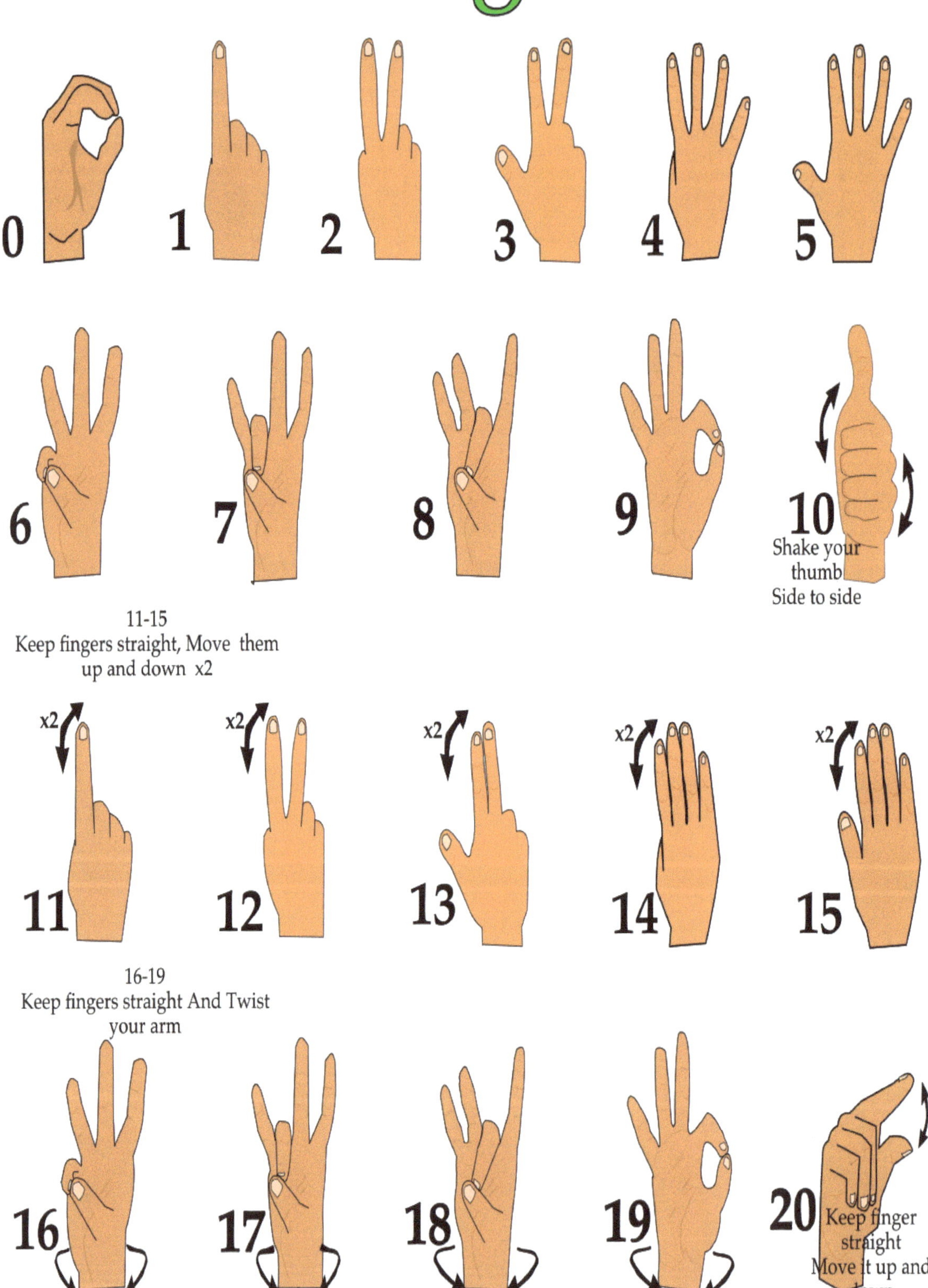

Foods
Set 1

Banana
Pretend to
Peel your finger
like a banana

Broccoli
Make a stem with one
hand and the tip of the
Broccoli with the other

Apple
Knuckle on your
cheek, rotate
back-and-forth

Cracker
Tap your fist
on your elbow

Orange
fist by your chin
open/close like
squeezing an orange

Grapes
Make your hand into a
claw and bounce it on
your other arm

These books are written by a mother and her children. The design of the books is focused on and directed by her 5 youngest children. The heart of these books is driven by the **love for children** and empowering them to explore their own creativity through interactive learning and using their own special talents and little people enthusiasm. Being a homeschooling mom with 9 special needs children, Eimiko believes in the beauty of the simple design which supports imagination, recognition of shapes, colors, numbers, animals, the natural world, and social environments.

This mom, and her children, are **passionate** about the writing of their books and **sharing** their stories, art and the wonder of communication through signing. In spite of their special needs, each of the children lives their lives in the freedom and true understanding they are not limited by anything but their beliefs. They believe they can do anything and learning to sign **since infancy** has fostered this belief and **empowered** them to see themselves as **vital and blessed** contributors to our world.

This mom is not just a writer, but seeks to be an inspiration with her books, as they are built on a foundation of love for Sign Language and children. Through the support of her friends and loved ones, these special books are now accessible for other families, schools, and most importantly children to enjoy.

Copyright © 2021 Eimiko Murlin
www.youtube.com/
eimikoscreations
Printed in the United States of America First Printing in 2021

This book is intended as an informational guide. The views expressed within are solely the opinions of the author, based on personal experience. The author, publisher, printer and all other parties involved deny any responsibility for injury to both body and property due to the misuse of information contained here in.

www.ingramcontent.com/pod-product-compliance
Lightning Source LLC
Chambersburg PA
CBHW042123110726
48006CB00003B/748